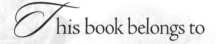

This book belongs to

_____

a mom after God's own heart.

GROWTH AND
STUDY GUIDE

A M♥M
After
God's Own
Heart

Elizabeth George

HARVEST HOUSE PUBLISHERS

EUGENE, OREGON

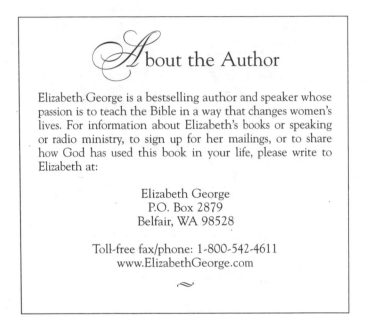

About the Author

Elizabeth George is a bestselling author and speaker whose passion is to teach the Bible in a way that changes women's lives. For information about Elizabeth's books or speaking or radio ministry, to sign up for her mailings, or to share how God has used this book in your life, please write to Elizabeth at:

Elizabeth George
P.O. Box 2879
Belfair, WA 98528

Toll-free fax/phone: 1-800-542-4611
www.ElizabethGeorge.com

A MOM AFTER GOD'S OWN HEART GROWTH AND STUDY GUIDE
Copyright © 2005 by Elizabeth George
Published by Harvest House Publishers
Eugene, Oregon 97402
www.harvesthousepublishers.com

ISBN-13: 978-0-7369-1573-1
ISBN-10: 0-7369-1573-7

Printed in the United States of America

05   06   07   08   09   10   11   12   / BP-CF /   10   9   8   7   6   5   4   3   2   1

Contents

Before You Begin...

♡

Dear Mom,

As you launch into each chapter of this very special growth and study guide designed to help you become the mom after God's own heart you long to be, please do these few things:

Open your book...and review the chapter in the book *A Mom After God's Own Heart*.

Open your Bible...and follow along through the scriptures to see for yourself what God has to say about being a mom.

Open your eyes...to God's message to you personally about being a parent, remembering prayer is essential.

Open your heart...to any changes God prompts you to make. Even if a section seems to be more for moms whose children are older or younger than yours, look for God's lessons to you in your situation.

Open your heart...to others. If you want to study with one or more other moms, you can find information for "Leading a Bible Study Discussion Group" on my website: **www.ElizabethGeorge.com.**

I'm praying for you!
Your friend and fellow mom in Christ,

Elizabeth George

Focusing on the Heart

In your copy of *A Mom After God's Own Heart,* read the opening chapter entitled "Focusing on the Heart." What meant the most to you as a mom?

Note several things that challenged you as a mother.

What information was new, and what was a fresh reminder for you as you seek to follow after God's heart in your parenting?

At the Heart of All Things

- Look at Matthew 15:18-19. What does Jesus teach about the importance of focusing on your heart?

- How does He say the state of one's heart is made evident?

- Read Proverbs 4:23. In the sidebar you read, "God begins molding a mother after His own heart on the inside—in the inner woman and her heart—and then works outward." What are God's instructions to you in this proverb about tending your heart, and why is it important to do so?

- What does Psalm 40:8 say about your heart, and how does it affect your life and your parenting? Also, write down one thing you can do today to better care for your heart.

Children with a Heart for God

Before we look at the lives—and moms—of several men and women of the Bible, list those you are already familiar with who began to follow after God at a young age. Share a few thoughts about them here.

Samuel —

- What impresses you most about:

    Samuel's early devotion to God as recorded in 1 Samuel 1:28 and 1 Samuel 2:11?

    Samuel's responses to God as he heard the voice of the Lord, recorded in 1 Samuel 3:4 and 10?

Samuel's mother, Hannah —

- What was Hannah's problem in 1 Samuel 1:2? How did she handle it in verse 10, and what does this teach you?

    How did God answer Hannah in verses 17-20, and how did Hannah respond to God's answer in verses 24-28?

- "A mother's greatest joy in having a child is to give that child fully and freely to God." As you read this sidebar thought, how do you see Hannah, a mom after God's own heart, doing this, and what can you do to follow her example?

David—

- How is David described in 1 Samuel 13:14 and Acts 13:22?

- As a "young lad" or youth, what skills and abilities do you see in David as recorded in these verses?

  1 Samuel 16:11,19 and 17:15—

  1 Samuel 16:16-18 and 23—

  1 Samuel 17:34-36—

  1 Samuel 17:48-50—

  What honor did God bestow upon this young man after His own heart in 1 Samuel 16:10-13?

David's ancestors—

- Read Ruth 4:21-22, Matthew 1:5-6, and Luke 3:31-32. Who made up David's lineage, and what do you know about any of them?

- "God works through faithful parents who, in spite of dark and difficult days, walk obediently with Him." David's ancestors remained faithful to God, contributing to generation after generation of men and women after God's heart. What difficulties have you encountered, and how does the truth of 2 Corinthians 12:9-10 help you to stay faithful as you mold the hearts of the next generation?

Daniel—

- What do you learn about the spiritual heritage of Daniel and his friends in Daniel 1:1-6?

  What do you witness in these youths regarding

  —their convictions in Daniel 1:5 and 8?

  —their prayer lives in Daniel 2:16-18?

  —their beliefs in Daniel 3:12-17 and 26-30?

Daniel's family—

- "From a godly homelife and upbringing, a child can learn how to live a godly life in a sinful world." What do Daniel 1:3 and 6 say about the family heritage of Daniel and his three friends?

- Godly parents taught and trained these children, who became captives in a heathen land, about God. What does Proverbs 22:6 say you, as a mom after God's own heart, are to faithfully do with and for your children?

Timothy—

- What do you learn about this young man after God's heart and his relationship with the apostle Paul in 1 Timothy 1:2?

- What do you learn about his character and ministry to and with Paul in Philippians 2:19-23?

Timothy's family—

- What do you learn about Timothy and

  —his father in Acts 16:1? (A note: "Greek" means he was an unbeliever.)

  —his mother, Eunice, in Acts 16:1?

  —his grandmother, Lois, in 2 Timothy 1:5?

  —the gift his mother and grandmother gave him in 2 Timothy 1:5?

- In your book you read, "Despite division within the home, Timothy's mother instilled in him a character of faithfulness that carried into adulthood."[1] How does the faithfulness of Eunice and Lois encourage and challenge your heart as you seek to raise children after God's own heart?

Mary—

- It was this young woman after God's heart, the mother of our Lord, who praised, "He who is mighty has done great things for me" (Luke 1:49). What were a few of those "great things" according to these verses?

  Luke 1:28 and 30—

  Luke 1:31-33—

  Luke 1:48—

- What else do we learn about Mary in Luke 1:27 and 34?

- How did Mary, a teen, respond to God's message to her through the angel Gabriel in Luke 1:38? What does her reply reveal about her heart, and how does her response instruct you?

Mary's family—

- Although the Bible does not give details about Mary's parents, what royal name do you recognize in verse 31 of her genealogy in Luke 3:23-38?

- Consider this thought: "The role of godly parents is to make sure the hearts and minds of their children are saturated with the Word of God." Then glance through Mary's "Magnificat" in Luke 1:46-55. What evidence do you find there that indicates Mary's tender young heart and mind were saturated with God's Word...that someone at home made sure Mary knew about God?

- What did Mary's son Jesus say about the heart in Matthew 12:34, and what evidence do you find in Mary's outpouring of worship (verses 46-55) that points to the content of Mary's heart and mind?

Heart Response

Review your notes about the children mentioned in this lesson. Write out one message each child and/or mom sends across the centuries from their hearts to yours, and note one way you can carry out their message in your mothering.

♡   Samuel—

♡   David—

♡   Daniel—

♡   Timothy—

♡   Mary—

A verse to hide in your heart...
*Keep your heart with all diligence,
for out of it spring the issues of life.*
PROVERBS 4:23

From a Dad's Heart

Read this section again in your book. What one most exciting insight about parenting would you like to share with your husband? With a friend?

Write down at least one way you will encourage your husband in his role as a dad this week.

As you consider the content of this lesson, how will you pray this week for yourself?

For your husband?

Little Choices
That Reap
Big Blessings

Write out the little choices suggested in your book in the space below. Also feel free to add others to your list.

1.

2.

3.

4.

5.

Which one challenged you most as a mom and why?

Which one encouraged you in a big way as a mom and why?

Which one do you want to give more attention to this week, and what specifically do you plan to do?

1

$\mathscr{T}$ake Time to Nurture Your Heart

 In your copy of *A Mom After God's Own Heart,* read the chapter entitled "Take Time to Nurture Your Heart." What meant the most to you as a mom?

Note several things that challenged you as a mother.

What information was new, and what was a fresh reminder for you as you seek to follow after God's heart in your parenting?

Getting Started

- What do these scriptures say about being a mom?

  Psalm 113:9—

  Psalm 127:3—

- How did these women view being a mom?

  Sarah, in Genesis 21:6—

  Rachel, in Genesis 30:1—

- Think about your children for a minute. What do they mean to you, and how do you see God blessing you through them?

  Write down a few of the joys your little and big ones bring to your heart. Spend some time thanking God. Then share what you wrote with your children.

- In the sidebar you read, "Prayer is the only way of becoming the mom God wants you to be." How do you think prayer can make a difference in a mom's busy, challenging life? In her heart as a mother?

It's All About Your Heart

- Read Deuteronomy 6, a portion of Moses' second giving of God's law. Jot down a few comments about Moses' message to God's people and to you.

- Count for yourself from your version of the Bible how many times Moses used the words *you* and *your* in Deuteronomy 6:4-9 and 12 and record it here.

  What conclusions can you draw regarding the importance of your heart and your responsibilities as a mom after God's own heart?

- Look again at Hannah's prayer in 1 Samuel 2:1-10. What evidences do you find that indicate Hannah had followed the instructions of Deuteronomy 6:5-6?

- Read Deuteronomy 6, verse 4. Throughout the ages, God's people have been called to put their trust in the one and only God. In your book you were asked, "Exactly where is your trust?" As you consider your heart, your lifestyle, and your commitments, where does it appear you have placed your trust, and how could you better trust the Lord?

- Read verse 5. What does this scripture indicate is Step 1 to being a mom after God's own heart?

  What do you learn here about the desired intensity and scope of your love for God?

- Read Deuteronomy 6, verse 6. According to this verse, what is Step 2 to being a mom after God's own heart?

  Can you think of several ways this can occur? List them here.

- Read verse 7. What does Moses say the overflow of a heart filled with God's Word should be?

  What are God's instructions to you concerning your children? Also write out the times and places mentioned and at least one way you can put God's plan into practice this next week.

- Read Deuteronomy 6, verse 8. What do you learn here about how closely you should keep God's Word to you?

- Read verse 9. What is yet another way Moses suggested for keeping God's Word at hand, as a permanent part of your daily home life? What is one way you can follow his instruction?

- In verses 10 and 11, God again states His plan to bring His people into the Promised Land. Read verse 12. How do you think paying attention to the instructions in verses 4-9 would serve to keep you—and God's people—from forgetting the Lord?

Taking Care of Business

- Think again about Moses' instructions to parents in Deuteronomy 6:4-12. Which of them are you already following?

  Which ones need improvement?

- In your book this summary statement regarding Deuteronomy 6:4-12 is quoted: "We are to love God, think constantly about his commandments, teach his commandments to our children, and live each day by the guidelines in his Word."[1] As you reflect on these words, can you see any specific ways God is leading you or areas where He is asking for change as you seek to be a mom after His heart? Make a note of them here, and seal them with a prayer.

Let the Transformation Begin!

- I shared honestly about the negative effects I have experienced in my parenting when I fail to take time to nurture my heart with God's Word. Share any ways you can relate or have found yourself...

    ...running on empty—

    ...heartless in your efforts—

    ...worldly in your ways and thinking—

    ...carnal or unspiritual in your manner—

- How would the truths of these scriptures counter-act the situations above?

    Philippians 1:9-11—

    Colossians 3:23—

    1 John 2:15-17—

    Galatians 5:16 and 22-23—

Strength for Each Stretching Day

- In the sidebar you read, "The degree of our spiritual strength will be in direct proportion to the time we spend in God's Word." What do the examples of these people teach you about seeking God's strength each day for your challenges as a mom?

  Genesis 19:27 —

  Psalm 5:3 —

  Psalm 63:1 —

  Mark 1:35 —

- "For top performance, refuel daily from God's Word." What do these scriptures say about strength for a believer?

  Ephesians 3:16 —

  Colossians 1:10-11 —

  How can you increase your time spent in God's Word, even in the smallest increment, so that "the word of Christ [will] dwell in you richly" (Colossians 3:16)?

Heart Response

As you review the contents of this chapter and its "Heart Response" section, write out three specific ways you can better nurture your heart in God's Word. What makes each of these activities important to you and to your children?

♥

♥

♥

A verse to hide in your heart...
Let the word of Christ
dwell in you richly in all wisdom.
COLOSSIANS 3:16

From a Dad's Heart

Read this section again in your book. What one most exciting insight about parenting would you like to share with your husband? With a friend?

Write down at least one way you will encourage your husband in his role as a dad this week.

As you consider the content of this lesson, how will you pray this week for yourself?

For your husband?

Little Choices That Reap Big Blessings

Write out the little choices suggested in your book in the space below. Also feel free to add others to your list.

1.

2.

3.

4.

5.

Which one challenged you most as a mom and why?

Which one encouraged you in a big way as a mom and why?

Which one do you want to give more attention to this week, and what specifically do you plan to do?

2

$\mathcal{T}$each Your Children God's Word

 In your copy of *A Mom After God's Own Heart,* read the chapter entitled "Teach Your Children God's Word." What meant the most to you as a mom?

Note several things that challenged you as a mother.

What information was new, and what was a fresh reminder for you as you seek to follow after God's own heart in your parenting?

The Starting Point for a Mom After God's Heart

- Write down some of your special childhood memories. This week thank God and your parents for these memories.

- What do these scriptures say about beginning in Christ?

  John 3:7—

  Romans 6:23—

  John 1:12—

  1 John 5:11-12—

  2 Corinthians 5:17—

If you have not reached the beginning point of a relationship with Jesus Christ, set up a time with a pastor, a Christian friend, or your Bible-study leader to discuss it.

• Share briefly about your current Bible-reading habits, remembering "he who teaches the Bible is never a scholar; he is always a student." For instance, when and where does your time in God's Word occur? Are you pleased with your habits? With the results? If not, why not?

What changes will you make to be spiritually refreshed and energized each day?

• How did the writers of these scriptures view the importance and power of God's Word?

Jeremiah 15:16—

Job 23:12—

2 Timothy 3:16-17—

2 Timothy 4:13—

- The ancient Talmud, commenting on the laws of Moses, asks and answers, "Who is best taught? He who has first learned from his mother." How do you see the faithful mom after God's own heart in Proverbs 31:1-9 instructing her young one?

  List some of the lessons she included.

- Refresh your memory by reading Deuteronomy 6:5-7 in your Bible. Then answer these questions for yourself:

  Who is to teach?

  Who are you to teach?

  What are you to teach?

  How are you to teach?

  When are you to teach?

  Where are you to teach?

Christian Education 101

- Continuing on with the theme of God's instructions in Deuteronomy 6 and the emphasis of this chapter, read the scriptures below. In your own words, what message is God sending to moms about teaching their children about God's Word and about life?

  Proverbs 1:8—

  Proverbs 6:20—

  Proverbs 31:1—

  Ephesians 6:4—

- Share briefly about what you are presently doing to teach your children. For instance, when and where does your time together in God's Word occur? Are you pleased with your plan? With the results? Why or why not?

  What changes will you make so this time with your children becomes a greater priority in your busy family's routine?

From the Cradle to the Grave

*   As mentioned in your book, "The life of a Jew is religious from the cradle to the grave. In the room occupied by the mother and her newborn infant the rabbi puts a paper containing Psalm 121 in Hebrew."[1] Read this psalm in your Bible. What are a few of the assurances in this "Song of Ascents" that was sung by pilgrims as they traveled to Jerusalem to worship?

*   What are the ages of your children?

    How are you living out "the cradle to the grave" principle of teaching God's Word diligently to your children, no matter what their ages? Be sure to write out any changes that need to be made.

"Whetting" a Child's Heart

• Again, read Deuteronomy 6:7. Then look up the word "whet" in a dictionary, and write the definition here.

• As you think about Moses' instructions in Deuteronomy 6:7, this concept of "whetting" a child's heart, and your calling to teach the Scriptures to your children, what do you think is involved? Or what are some ways to "whet" a child's heart with God's Word?

• Read 1 Peter 2:2. How could and should this imagery and precept apply to your children?

• Look now at Hebrews 5:12-14. How do you see the idea and benefits of "whetting" here?

- It is believed by Bible scholars that both Jochebed (Moses' mom) and Hannah (Samuel's mom)
  had about three years to "whet" their young
  boys before their little ones went to live with
  others.

  Regarding Moses, read Exodus 2:1-10. How do
  you see Moses' early religious instruction and
  training coming to fruition in Hebrews 11:24-29?

  Regarding Samuel, read 1 Samuel 1:20-28 and
  2:11 and 18. How do you see Samuel's early religious instruction and training coming to fruition
  in 1 Samuel 3:19-21?

- How do you think teaching God's Word to your
  children will or does make a difference in their
  lives?

Yes, but How?

- *Verbal instruction*—How is the precept of verbal instruction communicated in Deuteronomy 6:7?

  Can you think of several ways this could be done with your children?

- *Visual instruction*—Read Deuteronomy 6:8-9 again. How do these instructions point to visual instruction?

  How do you think visual reminders would prompt your children to remember "the unseen Guest in the house Whose presence should control and hallow all that is said and done in it"?[2]

  Can you think of several ways this could be done with your children?

Heart Response

As you review the contents of this chapter and its "Heart Response" section, write out three specific ways you can better teach God's Word to your children. What makes each of these activities important to you and to your children?

♡

♡

♡

A verse to hide in your heart...
Faith comes by hearing,
and hearing by the word of God.
ROMANS 10:17

From a Dad's Heart

Read this section again in your book. What one most exciting insight about parenting would you like to share with your husband? With a friend?

Write down at least one way you will encourage your husband in his role as a dad this week.

As you consider the content of this lesson, how will you pray this week for yourself?

For your husband?

Little Choices
That Reap
Big Blessings

Write out the little choices suggested in your book in the space below. Also feel free to add others to your list.

1.

2.

3.

4.

5.

Which one challenged you most as a mom and why?

Which one encouraged you in a big way as a mom and why?

Which one do you want to give more attention to this week, and what specifically do you plan to do?

3

Talk to Your Children About God

 In your copy of *A Mom After God's Own Heart,* read the chapter entitled "Talk to Your Children About God." What meant the most to you as a mom?

Note several things that challenged you as a mother.

What information was new, and what was a fresh reminder for you as you seek to follow after God's heart in your parenting?

Speak Up!

- How does the sidebar quote, "It takes dedicated parents to produce consecrated children" apply to moms as you consider the message of these verses?

  Deuteronomy 6:5—

  Deuteronomy 6:6-7—

- A verse we will review often in this study is Matthew 12:34. Read it now. How would you evaluate the content of your conversations with your children up to now? What are your favorite topics to talk about? Or what do you and your children seem to always end up talking about?

- Look again at 1 Samuel 2:1-10. These are the utterances that flowed out of Hannah's mouth... and heart. What do her words reveal about her heart? (And remember, little Samuel was probably by her side listening in!)

• Do your children think of you as a "preacher"? Why or why not? What can you do to be more vocal about God with them, to talk to them more about God?

• Paul constantly asked others to pray for him. Read several of his appeals in your Bible:

Ephesians 6:18-20—

Colossians 4:2-6—

How do Paul's "prayer requests" guide you regarding what you can pray for and what you should seek in your interactions with your children?

- Review these positive results that occur when you speak of God:

  —You honor and glorify God.

  —You obey His command to talk of Him to your children.

  —You are spiritually affected as you voice your heart for God and your knowledge of Him.

  —Your chances for affecting and infecting your family by your communication go sky-high!

  Choose one of the above and share how you have experienced it to be true in your life. Also choose one that causes you to desire to speak up more often.

Speak Up Day and Night

- Think about God's goodness, mercy, and faith-fulness. What does Lamentations 3:22-23 tell us about God's nature?

- How can a mom use the following opportunities as springboards for talking to her children about God?

  A sunset—

  A rainy day—

  A puppy—

  A flower—

  A peanut butter-and-jelly sandwich—

- "Spiritual and moral principles are best conveyed in the laboratory of life."[1] What occurrences in your daily life could prompt you to speak up about the things of God to your children?

- As you read the verses that follow in your Bible, note how they relate to your heart, to your thoughts, and to the content of your speech.

  Psalm 1:2-3—

  Psalm 19:1-11—

  How do you think meditating on God and His Word "day and night" would affect your "speaking up day and night"?

It's Never Too Early...

- Read Matthew 19:13-15. Briefly describe the scene. What was Jesus' desire for the children?

- How does the story of the teacher who started teaching a child at age two to play the violin affect your thinking about teaching spiritual things to your children...even at two years old?

- Read 2 Timothy 3:15-17. What wisdom should parents be sharing with their children "from childhood"?

What do you learn about the Word of God and its benefits in a heart and life, whether yours or your children's, and how does this encourage you to talk to your little ones about God today?

...And It's Never Too Late

- How do the statistics about children and religious matters motivate you to begin today to talk more freely and often to your children of all ages about God?

- Read Romans 10:14-15. Why is it important to begin today to constantly talk to your children about the things of God, regardless of their ages?

- Read Acts 16:25-31. Paul and Silas were very vocal about their faith in God. What was their impact and the result of their talking about God?

Speaking of the Lord can have the same affect on your children. What will you do today to be more vocal about your faith in God?

How Important Is God to You?

- Three key questions were asked in your book that are worth thinking about now:

    1. How important is God and His Son to you?
    2. How important is nurturing godly character in your life?
    3. Are you emulating God's standards to your family?

    Now read 1 Corinthians 11:1. How does this precept apply to these three questions regarding a mom's influence on her children?

- What encouragement can you derive from being reminded that it's never too late to commit to the priorities of God and His Word, to begin speaking up about your love for God?

Heart Response

As you review the contents of this chapter and its "Heart Response" section, write out three specific things you can do to ensure that you talk to your children about God. What makes each of these activities important to you and to your children?

♡

♡

♡

A verse to hide in your heart...
How beautiful are the feet of those
who preach the gospel of peace,
who bring glad tidings of good things!
ROMANS 10:15

From a Dad's Heart

Read this section again in your book. What one most exciting insight about parenting would you like to share with your husband? With a friend?

Write down at least one way you will encourage your husband in his role as a dad this week.

As you consider the content of this lesson, how will you pray this week for yourself?

For your husband?

Little Choices
That Reap
Big Blessings

Write out the little choices suggested in your book in the space below. Also feel free to add others to your list.

1.

2.

3.

4.

5.

Which one challenged you most as a mom and why?

Which one encouraged you in a big way as a mom and why?

Which one do you want to give more attention to this week, and what specifically do you plan to do?

4

$\mathcal{T}$ell Your Children About Jesus

In your copy of *A Mom After God's Own Heart,* read the chapter entitled "Tell Your Children About Jesus." What meant the most to you as a mom?

Note several things that challenged you as a mother.

What information was new, and what was a fresh reminder for you as you seek to follow after God's heart in your parenting?

Aim for Your Child's Heart

- Look up the word "ambassador" in a dictionary, and write out the definition here.

- Read 2 Corinthians 5:20 in your Bible. Who do you represent as a Christian?

  What is your function, and what does that mean based on the definition above?

  What is to be your message?

  What word(s) indicate Paul's passionate desire to get his message across to others?

  How does Paul's zeal to preach Christ motivate you when it comes to your children? Or how would you complete this sentence: "To better preach Christ to my children, I must..."

• In your book you were asked to think about your life and your heart as it relates to aiming the gospel message toward your child's heart. What has been the aim or focus of your parenting until now? Or what has been important to you so far in your child-raising?

• Read again 2 Timothy 3:14-15. What was the "aim" of mother and grandmother, Eunice and Lois, as they raised Timothy?

How does their dedication challenge you as you raise your children?

How does their dedication encourage you?

• How does the thought that "without Jesus, there is no life" motivate you to be more earnest in telling your children about the Lord Jesus?

Note at least one way you will adjust your aim to begin telling your children about Jesus daily.

Directing the Truths About Jesus

- "The birth of Jesus was the most important event in all of history." How should this statement affect what you say to your children about Jesus and how you live in front of them?

- What do the following scriptures teach about Jesus Christ?

  John 1:1 and 14—

  John 1:18—

  John 20:31—

  1 Timothy 2:5—

- What do the following scriptures teach about eternal life?

  John 1:12—

  John 11:25—

  John 14:6—

  1 John 5:11-13—

•   What do the following scriptures teach about telling your children about Jesus?

Romans 10:14-15—

2 Timothy 3:15—

•   "Faith in Jesus is the most important event in the history of a child's life." After reading the verses in this lesson and the suggestions given in your book for "Directing the Truths About Jesus," what will you do today and this week to direct the truths about Jesus toward your children's hearts?

Hitting the Bull's-Eye

- Look at John 1:1-5, and list some of the truths about Jesus found there.

  Verse 1—

  Verse 2—

  Verse 3—

  Verse 4—

  Verse 5—

  Continue on and list further truths about Jesus from these verses:

  Colossians 1:15—

  Colossians 1:17—

  Hebrews 12:2—

• Read again and write out the following verses dealing with the gospel.

Romans 3:23—

Romans 6:23—

John 1:12—

John 3:16—

• Write out an answer to your child's question, "Mom, how can I go to heaven?" When you are done, pray for opportunities to share your answer and the truth about Jesus.

• What can you as a mom do to "build a bridge of truth to your child's heart and pray for Jesus to walk over it"?

But What If...?

- From your observations, what do you think the level of spiritual understanding is for each of your children? Make notes for your eyes only.

- Write out several things you can do to encourage each child to the next level of spiritually understanding the truths of who Jesus is and what He has done for mankind.

When Should You Start?

- Is your child under five years old? Under seven years old? Read Charles Haddon Spurgeon's poem again on page 95 in your book, and write out a sentence or two stating your resolve to teach your children about Jesus.

Never Give Up!

There are three things a mom must do for her children of all ages.

- *Remember*—What is it you must remember about salvation?

  What do these scriptures have to say about this important truth?

  John 1:12-13—

  Acts 16:14—

  Romans 5:8—

  Ephesians 2:8-9—

- *Pray*—On a separate piece of paper, in your prayer journal, or in the back of your Bible write out a brief prayer for the salvation of your children. Date it, and pray it on a regular basis.

  Read Ephesians 6:18-20. Then, using Paul's example, write out a prayer for yourself too.

- *Talk*—What did Paul say about the gospel in Romans 1:16?

Pick a time to talk about Jesus with each of your children. Ask them to tell you what they understand about Jesus—about who He is and what He did for mankind. Do your best to fill in any voids in their comprehension and trust God with the results, always remembering the importance of a clear presentation of the truths of Jesus Christ. And don't be afraid or hesitant. Remember, "the gospel breaks hard hearts." Jot down some notes about what you will cover in future talks with your children.

Heart Response

As you review the contents of this chapter and its "Heart Response" section, write out three specific things you can do to ensure that you tell your children about Jesus. What makes each of these activities important to you and to your children?

♡

♡

♡

A verse to hide in your heart...
I am the way, the truth, and the life.
No one comes to the Father except through Me.
JOHN 14:6

From a Dad's Heart

Read this section again in your book. What one most exciting insight about parenting would you like to share with your husband? With a friend?

Write down at least one way you will encourage your husband in his role as a dad this week.

As you consider the content of this lesson, how will you pray this week for yourself?

For your husband?

Little Choices That Reap Big Blessings

Write out the little choices suggested in your book in the space below. Also feel free to add others to your list.

1.

2.

3.

4.

5.

Which one challenged you most as a mom and why?

Which one encouraged you in a big way as a mom and why?

Which one do you want to give more attention to this week, and what specifically do you plan to do?

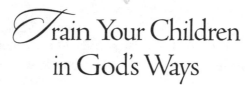

5

Train Your Children in God's Ways

In your copy of *A Mom After God's Own Heart,* read the chapter entitled "Train Your Children in God's Ways." What meant the most to you as a mom?

Note several things that challenged you as a mother.

What information was new, and what was a fresh reminder for you as you seek to follow after God's heart in your parenting?

Growing a Child

- Look up Proverbs 22:6 in your Bible, and write it here.

  What does Ephesians 6:4 add to your understanding of your role as a parent?

- *Educate*—Briefly scan this section in your book. What changes do you need to make as a mom in light of your role as educator?

- *Initiate*—Briefly scan this section in your book. What changes do you need to make as a mom in light of your role as initiator?

- Read Proverbs 29:15. What does it say generally happens to the child who is not trained in the way he should go?

• *Hands-on training*—List three ways you already give hands-on training to your children.

According to 2 Timothy 3:16-17, what is the end goal of godly training? How is this goal accomplished?

• *Live-it-out training*—Prayerfully read the verses below, and share what they teach concerning live-it-out training.

Proverbs 23:26—

1 Corinthians 4:16—

1 Corinthians 11:1—

Philippians 3:17—

Philippians 4:9—

In the sidebar you read, "Train up a child in the way he should go, and go that way yourself!"[1] Can you think of any changes that can be made in your daily life so your live-it-out training sends a stronger message of Christ to your child? Jot down one change here...and, with God's help and by His grace, make the change! Then enjoy again the poem on page 110 in your book.

From a Seedling

- Briefly scan the information given on Samuel and Timothy under "Children with a Heart for God," on pages 14-16 and 19-20. How do you see early training and instruction playing power-ful roles in the development of these two "seedlings"? Make notes here about what impresses you most about each child and what impresses you most about their mothers.

Samuel—

Timothy—

• Think about this: "The kind of person your child is going to be, he is already becoming...and becoming quickly!"² What can you do to nurture, cultivate, and train your children today, regardless of their ages?

Read through *Susannah's Rules for Rearing Children* on pages 125-126, and jot down two or three of her guidelines that gave you new insights into training your children or gave you ideas you would like to put into practice.

Remember this insight: "Let every father and mother realize that when their child is three years of age, they have done more than half they will ever do for its character."³

Which Way, Lord?

- Make notes about the "ways" mentioned in these verses:

  Proverbs 4:14-15—

  Proverbs 4:23-27—

  Proverbs 14:12—

  John 14:6—

- *God's way*—Why is it important for you to "train" and educate your child "in the way he should go," in God's way?

  Read Proverbs 4:10-13. What role did the parent play in this passage, and what assurances did he give to his child?

  Look at Proverbs 6:20-23. What role did the parents play in these verses, and what assurances did they give to their child?

• *God's wisdom*—Note some of God's wisdom below, reading each verse for yourself in your Bible. Jot down a few words concerning the message of each scripture.

Discipline the child in whom you delight (Proverbs 3:12)—

Discipline while there is hope (19:18)—

Discipline diligently the child you love (13:24)—

Discipline a child in the way he should go (22:6)—

Discipline foolishness out of your child's heart (22:15)—

Discipline evil out of your child's heart (20:30)—

Look back over these teachings from the Bible, and take a few minutes to evaluate your estimation of the importance of disciplining your children. Make a list of some specific ways you can be more consistent.

WARNING! What is the caution in Ephesians 6:4?

- *The child's way*—Read Proverbs 22:6 again. This verse has been translated, "Educate a child according to his life requirements," "train a child for his proper trade,"[4] and point him in "the way"—his way, "that way selected for him in which he should go."[5] As you think about the "bent" of each of your children, how can you encourage these individuals in their own "way"?

Harvesting the Fruit of Your Labors... and Love

- Read the story of "the prodigal son" in Luke 15:11-24. Briefly describe the son's actions.

  What does this parable communicate about the father's hope for his son?

  How do you see this young man's probable early training coming to fruition, and what hope does it give you as a parent?

- Describe the scene surrounding the faithful mom in Proverbs 31:28-31. How do you think she was blessed by her children?

  Based on these verses and verses 10 and 27, what kind of mom do you think she was?

10 Commands for Guiding Your Children

Read through this list on page 124, and look at each scripture in your Bible, making brief notes as you go.

♥   Teach them, using God's Word (Deuteronomy 6:4-9).

♥   Tell them what's right and wrong (1 Kings 1:6).

♥   See them as gifts from God (Psalm 127:3).

♥   Guide them in godly ways (Proverbs 22:6).

♥   Discipline them (Proverbs 29:17).

♥   Love them unconditionally (Luke 15:11-32).

♡   Do not provoke them to wrath (Ephesians 6:4).

♡   Earn their respect by example (1 Timothy 3:4).

♡   Provide for their physical needs (1 Timothy 5:8).

♡   Pass your faith along to them (2 Timothy 1:5).[6]

As you look back over this chapter and this list of ways to guide your children in God's direction, write your thoughts concerning your goal of training up your children in the way they should go. Don't forget to include some specific ways you can begin to do this.

As you review the contents of this chapter and its "Heart Response" section, write out three specific things you can do to ensure that you train your children in God's ways. What makes each of these activities important to you and to your children?

♡

♡

♡

A verse to hide in your heart...
*Train up a child in the way he should go,
and when he is old he will not depart from it.*
PROVERBS 22:6

From a Dad's Heart

Read this section again in your book. What one most exciting insight about parenting would you like to share with your husband? With a friend?

Write down at least one way you will encourage your husband in his role as a dad this week.

As you consider the content of this lesson, how will you pray this week for yourself?

For your husband?

Little Choices
That Reap
Big Blessings

Write out the little choices suggested in your book in the space below. Also feel free to add others to your list.

1.

2.

3.

4.

5.

6.

7.

Which one challenged you most as a mom and why?

Which one encouraged you in a big way as a mom and why?

Which one do you want to give more attention to this week, and what specifically do you plan to do?

6

Take Care of Your Children

 In your copy of *A Mom After God's Own Heart,* read the chapter entitled "Take Care of Your Children." What meant the most to you as a mom?

Note several things that challenged you as a mother.

What information was new, and what was a fresh reminder for you as you seek to follow after God's heart in your parenting?

What's for Dinner?

- Briefly describe a typical meal at your house—
  the menu, the setting, and the personal interaction.

  Breakfast—

  Lunch—

  Dinner—

  Mealtime is a fact of life. How are you presently
  handling this reality? And how would you rate
  your attitude on most days?

- Read these verses in Proverbs 31 that describe
  the "ideal" when it comes to the provision and
  preparation of food for the family, the atmos-
  phere in the home, and the nurturing of inter-
  personal relationships. It's from another era in
  time, but it paints a pretty picture of a mom's
  heart for her loved ones. Briefly, what do you
  see here?

  Verse 14—

  Verse 15—

Verse 16—

Verse 26—

Verse 27—

Verse 28—

Verse 29—

* What was Jesus' attitude toward feeding His followers in Mark 6:32-42? (Don't forget to contrast our Lord's attitude with that of His disciples.)

What was Jesus' attitude toward feeding His disciples in John 21:9-13?

- *"Tiger's milk"*—What is the principle given in Proverbs 30:8 regarding food?

How would you rate the nutritional value of the food you put in front of your children? Also, how would you rate your children's health and weight?

- *Get-up-and-go power*—Briefly read through 1 Samuel 14:24-32 with your family's food needs in mind. What happens at your house when a meal is late or missed or you're running errands with the family in the backseat and have no snacks?

- Read Matthew 6:11. What strikes you most about Jesus' words, and how can you pay more attention to doing this for your family?

- Check where your needs lie in the area of food in the "Tender Loving Care Department." I need to learn...

  ___ more about nutrition.

  ___ to plan ahead for meals and snacks.

  ___ to make a weekly menu.

  ___ to make a schedule for each day, meals included.

  ___ to factor in meal preparation time in my daily schedule.

- As you think about the importance of knowing "What's for Dinner," what steps for improvement will you take?

- With calendar in hand, pick a week when you will attempt to eat dinner together as a family for seven days in a row.

Will I Be Safe Today?

Think through the following areas of life where your children need protection. As you review these sections in your book, briefly write out what you are already doing to protect them and anything you still need to do. Be sure to look at the scriptures cited, and note how their principles relate to each area.

- *Protection from siblings*—John 13:34-35

- *Protection from accidents*—Philippians 2:3-4

- *Protection from incidents*—Matthew 10:16

- *Protection through education*—Matthew 6:13

- *Protection from the internet*—Psalm 101:3

- *Protection from TV*—Job 31:1

- *Protection from the opposite sex*—1 Corinthians 6:18,20

Why Do I Have to Rest?

- Read John 4:6. What do you learn here about Jesus in His humanity?

- Read Mark 6:31. What do you learn here about Jesus' awareness of His disciples' need for rest? What did He do about it?

- What can you do to eliminate or curtail whatever is interfering with your children getting their needed rest?

Heart Response

As you review the contents of this chapter and its "Heart Response" section, write out three specific things you can do to ensure that you take care of your children. What makes each of these activities important to you and to your children?

♡

♡

♡

A verse to hide in your heart...
She watches over the ways of her household,
and does not eat the bread of idleness.
PROVERBS 31:27

From a Dad's Heart

Read this section again in your book. What one most exciting insight about parenting would you like to share with your husband? With a friend?

Write down at least one way you will encourage your husband in his role as a dad this week.

As you consider the content of this lesson, how will you pray this week for yourself?

For your husband?

Little Choices That Reap Big Blessings

Write out the little choices suggested in your book in the space below. Also feel free to add others to your list.

1.

2.

3.

4.

5.

6.

7.

8.

Which one challenged you most as a mom and why?

Which one encouraged you in a big way as a mom and why?

Which one do you want to give more attention to this week, and what specifically do you plan to do?

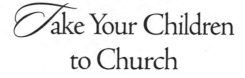

7

ℐake Your Children
to Church

In your copy of *A Mom After God's Own Heart,* read the chapter entitled "Take Your Children to Church." What meant the most to you as a mom?

Note several things that challenged you as a mother.

What information was new, and what was a fresh reminder for you as you seek to follow after God's heart in your parenting?

One Little Girl

- Take a minute or two to share your personal experiences of going to church, of not going to church, or of any religious exposure you received as a child.

- What were your thoughts about God, Jesus, the Bible, and church as you were growing up?

- "Please take me to Sunday school and church regularly...I enjoy learning more about God."[1] What impression does this sidebar quote from your book make on you regarding taking your children to church?

One Little Boy

- Now share what you know of your husband's experiences of going to church, of not going to church, or of any religious exposure he received as a child.

- Do you know what his thoughts about God, Jesus, the Bible, and church were as he was growing up? If not, casually ask him at a good time...and then just listen as he answers.

The Difference Church Can Make

- Read again about Moses' concern that the parents of future generations teach God's law in Deuteronomy 6:6-7. How have you improved in this area since you began your study of this book? What changes have been made at home?

- Read Deuteronomy 6:20-25. Moses was also concerned that the practice of proper worship be passed on to generation after generation. Do you share the same concern? Have your children ever asked why you go to church? How have you answered or would you answer?

- In your book you read this sidebar quote: "Putting God first puts a powerful example before our children." What kind of church-going example are you putting before your children? Again, do changes need to be made? If so, what changes?

- Enjoy again the "Generations of Excuses" at the end of your chapter. After reading through the variety of excuses listed, what difference could or does *not* taking your children to church make? Did you find yourself there? If so, what are you going to do about any of your excuses?

Jesus and Church

- Read Luke 2:41-50, and describe:

   Jesus' parents' faithfulness to worship (verse 41)—

   Jesus' journey to worship (verse 42)—

- What happened while Jesus was in Jerusalem fulfilling God's law that required His people to assemble regularly for worship (verses 43 and 46-49)?

- We noted that the Savior grew up in a home where God's laws were obeyed and the pre-scribed annual festivals were faithfully observed. Now think of your own precious children. Are they growing up going to church, or is this something you need to pay more attention to?

Why Is Church So Important?

- As you look at each of these scriptures in your Bible, count your blessings! What do these verses say about the experiences enjoyed at church?

  Colossians 4:16—

  1 Timothy 2:8—

  Matthew 26:30—

  1 Corinthians 16:2—

  Acts 2:42—

  Hebrews 10:24-25—

Again, remember, no church is perfect, and going to church does not make you a Christian. But good things will happen because of your obedience. And remember too this thought from John Wesley—"There is nothing more un-Christian than a solitary Christian."

Jesus' Take on Children

- Read Mark 10:13-16 in your Bible. Also read Luke 18:15-17. Compare the two passages and answer these questions:

    Who were the people present?

    What was happening in the scene?

- How did the disciples respond to the parents who brought their children to Jesus?

    How did Jesus respond to the parents—and to His disciples?

    Even though the disciples' intentions may have been good, why do you think Jesus was so indignant?

- What kind of heart do you think Jesus was referring to in Luke 18:17?

- Consider this thought from your book: "Are we helping or hindering children from coming to Christ? Are we, ourselves, receiving the kingdom of God with childlike trust?"[2] How do these passages relate to you as a parent?

How do these passages relate to you and your faith in Christ?

- What impressions do these two passages from Mark and Luke make on you regarding taking your children to church?

But What If...?

- Describe your own church-going situation. Do you have any "but what ifs," or other problems to deal with? How are you handling them? What have you learned that you could put into practice that might help your situation?

- What and how regularly are you praying about your family's church-going habits?

- What moms do you know who need encouragement as they deal with difficulties in taking their children to church, and how can you help?

Heart Response

As you review the contents of this chapter and its "Heart Response" section, write out three specific things you can do to ensure that you take your children to church. What makes each of these activities important to you and to your children?

♡

♡

♡

A verse to hide in your heart...
Let the little children come to Me,
and do not forbid them;
for of such is the kingdom of God.
LUKE 18:16

From a Dad's Heart

Read this section again in your book. What one most exciting insight about parenting would you like to share with your husband? With a friend?

Write down at least one way you will encourage your husband in his role as a dad this week.

As you consider the content of this lesson, how will you pray this week for yourself?

For your husband?

Little Choices That Reap Big Blessings

Write out the little choices suggested in your book in the space below. Also feel free to add others to your list.

1.

2.

3.

4.

5.

6.

Which one challenged you most as a mom and why?

Which one encouraged you in a big way as a mom and why?

Which one do you want to give more attention to this week, and what specifically do you plan to do?

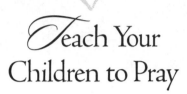

8

Ꮚⲓeach Your
Children to Pray

In your copy of *A Mom After God's Own
Heart,* read the chapter entitled "Teach Your
Children to Pray." What meant the most to
you as a mom?

Note several things that challenged you as a mother.

What information was new, and what was a fresh reminder for you as you seek to follow after God's heart in
your parenting?

The Optimum Mom

- Review your knowledge of Hannah's famous prayer by reading 1 Samuel 2:1-10. What impresses you about this prayer? Note several observations.

- Read 1 Samuel 3:3-20 to see how Samuel began "talking" to God. How did he respond to God's guidance in His life?

- In your book, review the content of some of Samuel's prayers listed in this chapter. What conclusions can you draw regarding his prayer life?

Other Praying Moms

- Do you have a preschooler? What effect did the illustration of the heathen mother teaching her little one to pray and worship have on you as a Christian mom?

- At what stage is your little one, and how skilled is he or she at prayer?

- What are you doing to teach your small-fry to pray?

- Do you have a teen? What were your thoughts as you read in your book that 91 percent of 13-year-olds pray to God during a typical week?[1]

- When you read about the teens who wished their parents had done a few things differently, were you surprised? Why or why not?

- How do you think your teen will one day look back on your spiritual input—or lack of it—especially in this key area of teaching them to pray?

- How does this sidebar quote motivate you to model a life of authentic prayer: "You cannot lift your children to a higher level than that on which you live yourself"?

- What instruction, structure, books, journals, and so forth, can you provide to help point your children toward personal prayer?

A Walk Through Your Day

- It's your turn to walk through a typical day at your house. In a few words, describe how you could bring prayer into...

breakfast time—

devotional time—

work or chore time—

leaving for school time—

homeschool lesson time—

homework time—

arriving home from school time—

snack time—

go to work time—

another mealtime—

bedtime—

Prompting Prayer

- Review the prayer prompts (the *Ask* questions) in your book. Which ones will work for your children at their ages?

- Review the method Mrs. Graham used in teaching her famous son, Billy Graham, to pray (found on page 177). How could you do something like this with your children?

- Think of your own prayer prompts, and note them here. Also, write out exactly when you will initiate or increase these methods of teaching your children to pray.

Praying Always...for All Things

- Look up the following scriptures in your Bible. What lesson does each convey about the importance of prayer?

  Ephesians 6:18—

  1 Thessalonians 5:17—

  James 5:16—

  Philippians 4:6—

  James 5:16—

  Acts 6:4—

- As you pray always and for all things with your children, here are a few things you can add to your prayer habits.

  Pray with their friends—Who are your children's best friends, and how can you incorporate prayer into your times together with them?

  Pray on the phone—Are your children old enough to use a phone, have a phone, to phone home? Then what will you do the next time they call? (And remember, a good general rule is to keep phone prayers very short and very sweet... unless there is a serious problem.) Could you say...

  "Let's thank God."
  "Let's pray about this."
  "I don't want to hang up until we pray."

What else might you say?

―――――― *Heart Response* ――――――

As you review the contents of this chapter and its "Heart Response" section, write out three specific things you can do to ensure that you are teaching your children to pray. What makes each of these activities important to you and to your children?

♡

♡

♡

A verse to hide in your heart...
One of His disciples said to Him,
"Lord, teach us to pray,
as John also taught his disciples."
LUKE 11:1

From a Dad's Heart

Read this section again in your book. What one most exciting insight about parenting would you like to share with your husband? With a friend?

Write down at least one way you will encourage your husband in his role as a dad this week.

As you consider the content of this lesson, how will you pray this week for yourself?

For your husband?

Little Choices That Reap Big Blessings

Write out the little choices suggested in your book in the space below. Also feel free to add others to your list.

1.

2.

3.

4.

5.

6.

Which one challenged you most as a mom and why?

Which one choices encouraged you in a big way as a mom and why?

Which one do you want to give more attention to this week, and what specifically do you plan to do?

9

$\mathcal{T}$ry Your Best

 In your copy of *A Mom After God's Own Heart,* read the chapter entitled "Try Your Best." What meant the most to you as a mom?

Note several things that challenged you as a mother.

What information was new, and what was a fresh reminder for you as you seek to follow after God's own heart in your parenting?

1. Know Who You Are

- How would you answer the question, Who am I?

- List all of the roles you must assume in your daily life.

- Read Ephesians 1:3-4 and John 1:12. How do these verses help you to better understand who you are in God's eyes?

- Read Titus 2:3-5. How do verses 4 and 5 help you to better understand who you are in God's eyes?

2. Know What It Is You Do

- What does Jesus have to say about what it is you are to do in Matthew 22:37?

  Once again, look at Titus 2:3-5. What does this passage have to say about what you are to do concerning your family and home?

- How do you think knowing who you are and what you are supposed to do gives you freedom and direction each day?

  How do you think this knowledge would help you structure your days? Your schedule? Your life?

•   Answering these questions will help you determine where you are and what it is you are to do.

Are you drifting along...perhaps even in the
wrong direction?

Have you set goals for yourself?

Have you gotten things straight with God?

Have you made the hard and important decisions?

3. Realize You Cannot Serve Two Masters

- Read Matthew 6:24 for yourself in your Bible. In the sidebar quote in your book you read, "Divided loyalties lead to diluted living." How do you think Jesus' principle of a singular loyalty versus divided loyalties applies to your role as a mom?

- Have you made a choice as to who it is you are to serve? What is your answer? If you cannot answer, how can you begin to pray about this important life decision?

4. Keep It Simple

- Look up the words "stress" and "stressful" in a dictionary, and write out some definitions here.

- Review the suggestions in your book for keeping it simple around the house. Which one applies most to your lifestyle? Are there others you could add to the list?

- What can you do to keep it simple, steady as she goes, and not lose sight of the goal—of being a mom after God's own heart?

5. Don't Go It Alone

- Read Luke 1:39-45. How did the older woman, Elizabeth, encourage the younger woman, Mary?

- Read Philippians 2:19-22 and 1 Timothy 1:2 and 2 Timothy 1:2. How do these verses describe the bond between Paul and his young disciple Timothy?

- Do you have an older sister in the Lord you can turn to for advice, encouragement, and prayer support? If so, be sure and express your appreciation to her. If not, begin praying for God to lead you to the right person. In the meantime, don't hesitate to ask the older women you admire for advice on being a mom. What questions will you ask? Who might you call?

6. Take One Day at a Time

- Read Matthew 6:34 in your Bible. What three steps does Jesus give for taking one day at a time?

  Jesus' command—

  Jesus' conclusion—

  Jesus' challenge—

- Read Psalm 113:9. Are you in a hurry to have the present season of your life pass? Are you wishing away the tasks and responsibilities that make up your days as a mom? What can you do to change your attitude and be the "joyful mother of children" God means you to be?

- In your book you were encouraged to focus on making today count, to try your best to be the best mom you can be...just for today, to give mothering your all each and every day. How can you "sow your best efforts today" so you can "reap God's abundant blessings tomorrow"?

———— *Heart Response* ————

As you review the contents of this chapter and its "Heart Response" section, write out three specific things you can do to ensure that you try your best as a mom. What makes each of these activities important to you and to your children?

♡

♡

♡

A verse to hide in your heart...
And whatever you do, do it heartily,
as to the Lord and not to men.
COLOSSIANS 3:23

From a Dad's Heart

Read this section again in your book. What one most exciting insight about parenting would you like to share with your husband? With a friend?

Write down at least one way you will encourage your husband in his role as a dad this week.

As you consider the content of this lesson, how will you pray this week for yourself?

For your husband?

Little Choices That Reap Big Blessings

Write out the little choices suggested in your book in the space below. Also feel free to add others to your list.

1.

2.

3.

4.

5.

6.

7.

Which one challenged you most as a mom and why?

Which one encouraged you in a big way as a mom and why?

Which one do you want to give more attention to this week, and what specifically do you plan to do about it?

10

Talk to God About Your Children

 In your copy of *A Mom After God's Own Heart,* read the chapter entitled "Talk to God About Your Children." What meant the most to you as a mom?

Note several things that challenged you as a mother.

What information was new, and what was a fresh reminder for you as you seek to follow after God's own heart in your parenting?

The Whole Child

- Read Colossians 1:9-11, and chart or note the content of Paul's prayers for these believers.

  Read Philippians 1:6 and verses 9-11, and chart or note the content of Paul's prayers for these believers.

  How did Paul close his letter to the Thessalonians in 1 Thessalonians 5:23?

- What kind of prayer list could you make for your children based on Paul's prayers for his "children" in the faith?

- Read Ephesians 6:12. Why is it important to not only teach, train, and take care of your children but to also pray for them?

1. Pray for Your Child's Salvation

- In your book you read this sidebar quote: "Who better to pray for a child's second birth than the mom who gave birth to that child?" Recall or recount in a few words your own "baby story" surrounding the birth of each of your children.

- Now share about your prayers for their second birth, their spiritual birth, their salvation through Jesus Christ, their heart response to the gospel message. For instance, when do you pray? How often? Do you have a prayer page for each child? A prayer journal?

• How can you upgrade your prayer efforts? What can you do to be better organized, to make sure you pray for your child's salvation, that you lift "the whole child" before God regularly and consistently?

• Read Acts 16:14 in your Bible. Then write out your own "Lydia Prayer," using the prayer in your book and filling in the blank with your children's names.

• In the chapter in your book entitled "Tell Your Children About Jesus," you read about Monica, the praying mother of Augustine. Read about her again on pages 96-97. List several lessons her faithful prayer ministry for her child teaches you. When it comes to praying for the gracious salvation of our children, "may each of us be saved from the sin of prayerlessness!"[1]

2. Pray for Your Child's Friends

* Read 1 Corinthians 15:33 in your Bible. How does this principle of influence guide you as you pray for your child's friends?

  Read Proverbs 22:24-25 in your Bible. How does this principle of influence guide you as you pray for your child's friends?

* Read Psalm 1:1-2 in your Bible. Then write out your own "Psalm 1" prayer, using the prayer in your book and filling in the blank with your children's names.

* How can you better pray for your child's friendships and friends? Again, do you need to be more organized? Allot more time in your day to prayer? Find out more about his or her friends? Do whatever it takes, remembering, "Anyone who pushes you nearer to God is your friend."

3. Pray for Your Child's Purity

* Read 1 Thessalonians 4:3-7 in your Bible. Then note which verses teach the following facts.

   God has revealed His will concerning sexual purity—

   Steer clear of all sexual sin—

   It is possible to control your body—

   God's standards are the opposite of the world's—

   Sexual expression is reserved for marriage—

   Never tempt, tease, or take advantage of anyone sexually—

   We are called to holiness, and God will help us fulfill this calling—

• What did you learn about sexual purity that you can share with—and pray for—your child?

• Fill in the blank in this prayer for purity and pray it often:

> Lord, I pray that [your child's name] _____
> will keep himself (herself) from all sexual sin, that he (she) will learn how to master his (her) own body in holiness and purity, that he (she) will not succumb to temptation or take advantage of another person, that he (she) will understand that God has called us to dedicate ourselves to holiness and the most thorough purity.

4. Pray for Your Child's Schoolwork

*   What do these scriptures teach about a strong work ethic and the importance of doing all things well—including schoolwork?

    Proverbs 14:15—

    Proverbs 31:13—

    Ecclesiastes 9:10—

    Colossians 3:17—

    Colossians 3:23-24—

*   How does Proverbs 22:6 apply to directing your child's educational growth?

*   How can you better pray for your child's schoolwork? Do you need a special page in your prayer notebook? Are you including his or her teachers? Are you praying about future educational expenses? Make notes here, and be sure you are at least praying, "Lord, whatever _____ does, including his (her) schoolwork, motivate him (her) to do it heartily, as to the Lord and not to men."

5. Pray for Your Child's Church Involvement

- To refresh yourself, briefly turn through the chapter in your book entitled "Take Your Children to Church." Note any progress or changes you've made since reading that chapter.

- Read 2 Peter 3:18. Note several things it teaches about spiritual growth.

- Read Ephesians 4:15. Note several things it teaches about spiritual growth.

- Then fill in the blank with your children's names.

   Lord, may _____
   grow in the grace and knowledge of our Lord and Savior,
   Jesus Christ. May he (she)
   grow up in all things into
   Him who is the head—Christ.

Heart Response

As you review the contents of this chapter and its "Heart Response" section, write out three specific things you can do to ensure that you talk to God regularly about your children. What makes each of these activities important to you and to your children?

♡

♡

♡

A verse to hide in your heart...
And this I pray,
that your love may abound still more and more
in knowledge and all discernment.
PHILIPPIANS 1:9

From a Dad's Heart

Read this section again in your book. What one most exciting insight about parenting would you like to share with your husband? With a friend?

Write down at least one way you will encourage your husband in his role as a dad this week.

As you consider the content of this lesson, how will you pray this week for yourself?

For your husband?

Little Choices That Reap Big Blessings

Write out the little choices suggested in your book in the space below. Also feel free to add others to your list.

1.

2.

3.

4.

5.

6.

Which one challenged you most as a mom and why?

Which one encouraged you in a big way as a mom and why?

Which one do you want to give more attention to this week, and what specifically do you plan to do?

$\mathscr{M}$aking the Choices That Count

In your copy of *A Mom After God's Own Heart,* read the chapter entitled "Making the Choices That Count." What meant the most to you as a mom?

Note several things that challenged you as a mother.

What information was new, and what was a fresh reminder for you as you seek to follow after God's own heart in your parenting?

The Results of One Little Wrong Choice

- "Little choices determine habit; habit carves and molds character which makes the big decisions." Read Genesis 13:5-13 and list the choices Abraham made and those Lot made. Then write out the results and consequences of their choices as stated in Genesis 13:14-18 and 19:29.

  Abraham—

  Lot—

Making the Right Choices

- "History is made every time you make a decision." What right—and hard—choices did these women and moms in the Bible make?

  Jochebed in Exodus 1:22 and 2:1-3—

  Rahab in Joshua 2:1-4—

  Hannah in 1 Samuel 1:10-11,24-28, and 2:11—

- How do the following scriptures affirm God's promises to guide you as you seek to make the right choices?

  Psalm 32:8—

  Psalm 48:14—

  Proverbs 3:6—

  Proverbs 16:9—

- How does Joshua's heart—and choice—in Joshua 24:15 encourage and inspire you to make the right choices?

Choose to Put Your Personal Dreams on Hold

• What are your personal dreams? Take a few minutes to briefly jot them down. Every woman and mom has them. We all have special talents and abilities just waiting to blossom and be put to use. Share yours here.

• However, "life is not the result of dreams dreamed, but of choices made." Read Titus 2:3-5 again. Where does God say you are to put your efforts at this time or season in your life?

• Read Ecclesiastes 3:1-8. What does the message of this passage say regarding the best attitude to have toward life?

How does this encourage you to concentrate on doing the right things at the right time in your life?

Choose to Put First People First

- Look again at Titus 2:3-5. What does God say is the priority order of the people in your life?

- As a mom (like Hannah and Jochebed), what can you do to pour your efforts and energies into your children's lives today? To give your all to being a mom today, realizing that today is all you have?

    Think about C.H. Spurgeon's words, "Take care of your lambs, or where will you get your sheep from?" How do you think your care today will advance the maturity of your children—your lambs—tomorrow?

Choose to Be Mentored

- Once more read Titus 2:3-5, specifically verse 3.

  What kind of woman is mentioned here?

  What kind of woman is she to be?

  What kind of ministry is she to have?

- Do you have such a woman in your life? If not,
  How will you begin to pray?—

  Where will you begin to look?—

  Who will you approach?—

  What specific help do you desire?—

  Is there an organization you can join?—

Choose to Read Proverbs

- In your book you read this sidebar quote: "Your level of maturity is in direct proportion to your ability to make wise decisions." What does Proverbs 1:1-4 say the benefits of reading Proverbs will be?

  What does Proverbs 1:5-6 say about gaining wisdom and making wise decisions?

- Not only do you want to teach wisdom to your children, but you as a mom need God's wisdom. How do these proverbs indicate you can walk in wisdom?

  Proverbs 3:5-6—

  Proverbs 5:1-2—

  Proverbs 9:10—

  Proverbs 19:20—

Choose to Study the Moms in the Bible

- In this study you have come face-to-face with a number of moms in the Bible. Take a few minutes to recall the lessons you have learned from these noble mothers.

Jochebed, the mother of Moses—

Hannah, the mother of Samuel—

The Proverbs 31:10-31 mother—

Eunice and Lois, the mother and grandmother of Timothy—

Mary, the mother of Jesus—

Heart Response

As you review the contents of this chapter and its "Heart Response" section, write out three specific things you can do to ensure that you are making the choices that count. What makes each of these activities important to you and to your children?

♡

♡

♡

A verse to hide in your heart...
Trust in the LORD with all your heart,
and lean not on your own understanding;
in all your ways acknowledge Him,
and He shall direct your paths.
PROVERBS 3:5-6

From a Dad's Heart

Read this section again in your book. What one most exciting insight about parenting would you like to share with your husband? With a friend?

Write down at least one way you will encourage your husband in his role as a dad this week.

As you consider the content of this lesson, how will you pray this week for yourself?

For your husband?

A Final Choice for a Mom's Heart

- Look again at the list of godly, biblical attitudes for a mom's heart on page 247. As you look up the scriptures now, note one way you will seek to choose the attitudes God desires in you.

  Heartily: Colossians 3:23—

  Faithfully: 1 Timothy 3:11—

  Willingly: Proverbs 31:15—

  Excellently: Proverbs 31:29—

  Joyfully: 1 Thessalonians 5:16—

  Prayerfully: 1 Thessalonians 5:17—

  Thankfully: 1 Thessalonians 5:18—

Pray daily to become this mom—a mom after God's own heart, the mom you long to be!

$\mathcal{R}$eflections from Your Heart

Throughout this book you have entertained a number of "little choices that reap big blessings." As you review the weeks that have passed since you began this study about being a mom after God's own heart, what is the one most significant change or choice you have made in your parenting? How has your choice blessed you? Your children? Your home life? Write your answer below, enjoy the progress you have made, and thank God for His love and grace.

Notes

Focusing on the Heart

1. Michael Kendrick and Daryl Lucas, *365 Life Lessons from Bible People* (Wheaton, IL: Tyndale House Publishers, Inc., 1996), p. 355.

1 — Take Time to Nurture Your Heart

1. *Life Application Study Bible* (Wheaton, IL: Tyndale House Publishers, Inc., 1996), p. 269.

2 — Teach Your Children God's Word

1. G.M. Mackie, *Bible Manners and Customs* (Old Tappan, NJ: Fleming H. Revell Co., n.d.), p. 158.
2. Ibid., p. 159.

3 — Talk to Your Children About God

1. Sid Buzzell, *The Leadership Bible* (Grand Rapids, MI: Zondervan Publishing House, 1998), p. 207.

5 — Train Your Children in God's Ways

1. Eleanor Doan, *Speaker's Sourcebook* (Grand Rapids, MI: Zondervan Publishing House, 1988), p. 48.
2. Ibid., citing Heart to Heart Program, p. 49.
3. Ibid., quoting Horace Bushnell, p. 49.
4. Curtis Vaughan, *The Word: The Bible from 26 Translations*—citing *The New American Bible* and James Moffatt, *A New Translation of the Bible,* respectively (Gulfport, MS: Mathis Publishers, Inc., 1991), p. 1221.
5. Robert Jamieson, A.R. Fausset, and David Brown, *Commentary on the Whole Bible* (Grand Rapids, MI: Zondervan Publishing House, 1971), p. 470.
6. J. David Branon, as cited in Roy B. Zuck, *The Speaker's Quote Book* (Grand Rapids, MI: Kregel Publications, 1977), p. 51.

7 — Take Your Children to Church

1. "A Child's Ten Commandments to Parents," by Dr. Kevin Leman, from *Getting the Best out of Your Kids* (Eugene, OR: Harvest House Publishers, 1992.) Quoted in Alice Gray, Steve Stephens, John Van Diest, *Lists to Live By for Every Caring Family* (Sisters, OR: Multnomah Publishers, 2001), p. 130.
2. Bruce B. Barton, *Life Application Bible Commentary—Mark* (Wheaton, IL: Tyndale House Publishers, Inc., 1994), p. 285.

8 — Teach Your Children to Pray

1. George Barna survey results, *Transforming Children into Spiritual Champions* (Ventura, CA: Regal Books/Gospel Light, 2003), p. 35.

10 — Talk to God About Your Children

1. Herbert Lockyer, *All the Prayers of the Bible* (Grand Rapids, MI: Zondervan Publishing House, 1973), p. 64.

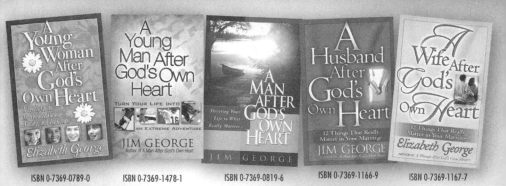